I0411965

SNIPPETS OF BARACK OBAMA

DAVE FARNHAM

ISBN-13: 978-1508477013
ISBN-10: 1508477019

Other books by Dave Farnham

Snippets of Nigel Farage

Snippets of Boris Johnson

Snippets of Richard Attenborough

Snippets of Paul Gascoigne

Snippets of Jeremy Kyle

Snippets of Joan Rivers

Snippets of Billy Connolly

Snippets of Marilyn Monroe

Snippets of Benjamin Franklin

Snippets of Oscar Wilde

Snippets of Abraham Lincoln

Snippets of Success

Snippets of Vladimir Putin

Snippets of Love

CONTENTS

INTRODUCTION

November 4th 2008 was an historic day for both the United States of America and, by implication, the rest of the world. On that date, Barack Hussein Obama was elected to be the nation's 44th President, the first ever African-American to take up that illustrious position. After the hopelessness of the years of the Bush administration, years marked by events such as the Twin Towers (9/11) horror, Hurricane Katrina's near-destruction of New Orleans and the worldwide recession, Obama's accession to the Presidency was seen as a turning point for America, a resurgence of hope, spelt out clearly in his slogan, "Yes, we can!"

The son of a Kenyan father and American mother, he was a graduate of Harvard Law School, proud of his roots and committed to equality of opportunity regardless of ethnic origins.

Obama's policies were the polar opposite of those of his predecessor: opposition to the war in Iraq, a wish to modify the Gun Laws, a striving towards greater equality of wealth and, above all, a desire to give all Americans access to healthcare regardless of their ability to pay.

As with so many Presidents before him, Barack Obama's aspirations were not shared by everyone and his opponents constantly put obstructions in his way. His standing among Americans began to drop, though in the rest of the world his popularity has remained markedly higher than that of George Bush Jr, with an equally improved international respect for his country.

So just who is Barack Hussein Obama and what makes him tick? In this book of his own words, you can begin to find the answer.

ABOUT HIMSELF & THE PRESIDENCY

"I always believe that ultimately, if people are paying attention, then we get good government and good leadership. And when we get lazy as a democracy and civically start taking shortcuts, then it results in bad government and politics."

*

"In a country of 300 million people there is a certain degree of audacity required for anybody to say 'I'm the best person to lead this country.'"

*

"I would put our legislative and foreign policy accomplishments in our first two years against any President - with the possible exceptions of Johnson, FDR, and Lincoln - just in terms of what we've gotten done in modern history. But, you know, but when it comes to the economy, we've got a lot more work to do. And we're gonna keep on at it."

*

"Over the last 15 months, we've traveled to every corner of the United States. I've now been in 57 states? I think one left to go."

*

"I cannot swallow whole the view of Lincoln as the Great Emancipator."

*

"If you're looking for the safe choice, you

shouldn't be supporting a black guy named Barack Obama to be the next leader of the free world."

*

"I just want to go through Central Park and watch folks passing by. Spend the whole day watching people. I miss that."

*

"Since I'm the President and Democrats have controlled the House and the Senate, it's understandable that people are saying, you know, 'What have you done?'"

*

"I just miss - I miss being anonymous."

*

"My identity might begin with the fact of my race, but it didn't, couldn't end there. At least, that's what I would choose to believe."

*

"To avoid being mistaken for a sellout, I chose my friends carefully. The more politically active black students. The foreign students. The Chicanos. The Marxist professors and structural feminists and punk-rock performance poets."

*

"And I will do everything that I can as long as I am President of the United States to remind the American people that we are one nation under God, and we may call that God different names but we remain one nation."

*

"There is probably a perverse pride in my administration... that we were going to do the right thing, even if short-term it was unpopular. And I think anybody who's occupied this office has to remember that success is determined by an intersection in policy and politics and that you can't be neglecting of marketing and P.R. and public opinion."

*

"If the critics are right that I've made all my

decisions based on polls, then I must not be very good at reading them."

*

"That's the good thing about being President, I can do whatever I want."

*

"The future rewards those who press on. I don't have time to feel sorry for myself. I don't have time to complain. I'm going to press on."

*

"Why can't I just eat my waffle?"

"The fact that my 15 minutes of fame has extended a little longer than 15 minutes is somewhat surprising to me and completely baffling to my wife."

*

"I found this national debt, doubled, wrapped in a big bow, waiting for me as I stepped into the Oval Office."

*

"You know, one of the things I think you understand as President is you're held responsible for everything, but you don't always have control of everything, right?"

*

"I miss Saturday morning, rolling out of bed, not shaving, getting into my car with my girls, driving to the supermarket, squeezing the fruit, getting my car washed, taking walks."

*

"My job is not to represent Washington to you, but to represent you to Washington."

*

"I've got a pen and I've got a phone - and I can use that pen to sign executive orders and take executive actions and administrative actions that move the ball forward."

*

"As President, I'm committed to making Washington work better and rebuilding the trust of the people who sent us here."

*

"I have Muslim members of my family. I have lived in Muslim countries."

*

"We need somebody who's got the heart, the empathy, to recognize what it's like to be a young teenage mom, the empathy to understand what it's like to be poor or African-American or gay or disabled or old - and that's the criterion by which I'll be selecting my judges."

"The day I'm inaugurated, this country looks at itself differently and the world looks at America differently. If you believe that we've got to heal America and we've got to repair our standing in the world, then I think my supporters believe that I am a messenger who can deliver that message around the world in a way that no other candidate can do."

*

"Let me even say before I even get inaugurated, during the transition we are going to be having meetings all across the country with community organizations so that you have input into the agenda for the next presidency of the United States of America."

*

"I consider it part of my responsibility as President of the United States to fight against negative stereotypes of Islam wherever they appear."

*

"I believe in American exceptionalism, just as I suspect that the Brits believe in British exceptionalism and the Greeks believe in Greek exceptionalism."

*

"But what we can do, as flawed as we are, is still see God in other people, and do our best to help them find their own grace. That's what I strive to do, that's what I pray to do every day."

"I'm a Christian by choice."

*

"So while an incredible amount of progress has been made, on this fifth anniversary, [of Hurricane Katrina] I wanted to come here and tell the people of this city directly: My administration is going to stand with you - and fight alongside you - until the job is done. Until New Orleans is all the way back, all the way."

*

"And we have done more in the two and a half years that I've been in here than the previous 43 Presidents to uphold that principle, whether it's ending 'don't ask, don't tell,' making sure that gay and lesbian partners can visit each other in hospitals, making sure that federal benefits can be provided to same-sex couples."

*

"What I think is fair to say is that, coming out of the Republican camp, there have been efforts to suggest that perhaps I'm not who I say I am when it comes to my faith - something which I find deeply offensive, and that has been going on for a pretty long time."

*

"Let me be absolutely clear. America is a strong friend of Israel's. It will be a strong friend of Israel's under a McCain administration. It will be a strong friend of Israel's under an Obama administration. So that policy is not going to change."

"You know, my faith is one that admits some doubt."

*

"If everybody that voted in 2008 shows up in 2010, we will win this election. We will win this election."

*

"My family, frankly, they weren't folks who went to church every week. My mother was one of the most spiritual people I knew but she didn't raise me in the church, so I came to my Christian faith later in life and it was because the precepts of Jesus Christ spoke to me in terms of the kind of life that I would want to lead."

"I'm inspired by the people I meet in my travels – hearing their stories, seeing the hardships they overcome, their fundamental optimism and decency. I'm inspired by the love people have for their children. And I'm inspired by my own children, how full they make my heart. They make me want to work to make the world a little bit better. And they make me want to be a better man."

*

"Even when folks are hitting you over the head, you can't stop marching. Even when they're turning the hoses on you, you can't stop."

*

"My task over the last two years hasn't just been to stop the bleeding. My task has also been to try to figure out how do we address some of the structural problems in the economy that have prevented more Googles from being created."

*

"Issues are never simple. One thing I'm proud of is that very rarely will you hear me simplify the issues."

*

"I will never forget that the only reason I'm standing here today is because somebody, somewhere stood up for me when it was risky. Stood up when it was hard. Stood up when it wasn't popular. And because that somebody stood up, a few more stood up. And then a few thousand stood up. And then a few million stood up. And standing up, with courage and clear purpose, they somehow managed to change the world."

*

"I'm happy to get good ideas from across the political spectrum, from Democrats and Republicans. What I won't do is return to the failed theories of the last eight years that got us into this fix in the first place, because those theories have been tested, and they have failed. And that's what part of the election in November was all about."

*

"I'm no longer just a candidate. I'm the President. I know what it means to send young Americans into battle, for I have held in my arms the mothers and fathers of those who didn't return. I've shared the pain of families who've lost their homes, and the frustration of workers who've lost their jobs."

Dave Farnham

ABOUT AMERICA

"Let's remember that our leadership is defined not just by our defense against threats, but by the enormous opportunities to do good and promote understanding around the globe - to forge greater cooperation, to expand new markets, to free people from fear and want. And no one is better positioned to take advantage of those opportunities than America."

*

"America can do whatever we set our mind to. That is the story of our history, whether it's the pursuit of prosperity for our people, or the struggle for equality for all our citizens; our commitment to stand up for our values abroad, and our sacrifices to make the world a safer place. Let us remember that we can do these things not just because of wealth or power, but because of who we are: one nation, under God, indivisible, with liberty and justice for all."

"In the unlikely story that is America, there has never been anything false about hope."

*

"There are a whole lot of religious people in America, including the majority of Democrats. When we abandon the field of religious discourse—when we ignore the debate about what it means to be a good Christian or Muslim or Jew; when we discuss religion only in the negative sense of where or how it should not be practiced, rather than in the positive sense of what it tells us about our obligations toward one another; when we shy away from religious venues and religious broadcasts because we assume that we will be unwelcome—others will fill the vacuum. And those who do are likely to be those with the most insular views of faith, or who cynically use religion to justify partisan ends."

"I don't want to pit Red America against Blue America. I want to be President of the United States of America."

*

"The true test of the American ideal is whether we're able to recognize our failings and then rise together to meet the challenges of our time. Whether we allow ourselves to be shaped by events and history, or whether we act to shape them. Whether chance of birth or circumstance decides life's big winners and losers, or whether we build a community where, at the very least, everyone has a chance to work hard, get ahead, and reach their dreams."

*

"No other country in the world does what

we do. On every issue, the world turns to us, not simply because of the size of our economy or our military might - but because of the ideals we stand for, and the burdens we bear to advance them."

*

"America is a land of big dreamers and big hopes. It is this hope that has sustained us through revolution and civil war, depression and world war, a struggle for civil and social rights and the brink of nuclear crisis. And it is because our dreamers dreamed that we have emerged from each challenge more united, more prosperous, and more admired than before."

*

"We, the People, recognize that we have

responsibilities as well as rights; that our destinies are bound together; that a freedom which only asks what's in it for me, a freedom without a commitment to others, a freedom without love or charity or duty or patriotism, is unworthy of our founding ideals, and those who died in their defense."

*

"The United States is not, and never will be, at war with Islam."

*

"Americans... still believe in an America where anything's possible - they just don't think their leaders do."

"In a world of complex threats, our security and leadership depends on all elements of our power - including strong and principled diplomacy."

*

"One of the great strengths of the United States is... we have a very large Christian population - we do not consider ourselves a Christian nation or a Jewish nation or a Muslim nation. We consider ourselves a nation of citizens who are bound by ideals and a set of values."

*

"What I believe unites the people of this nation, regardless of race or region or party, young or old, rich or poor, is the simple, profound belief in opportunity for all - the notion that if you work hard and take responsibility, you can get ahead."

*

"There are patriots who opposed the war in Iraq and there are patriots who supported the war in Iraq. We are one people, all of us pledging allegiance to the stars and stripes, all of us defending the United States of America."

*

"What Washington needs is adult supervision."

*

"I think what you're seeing is a profound recognition on the part of the American people that gays and lesbians and transgender persons are our brothers, our sisters, our children, our cousins, our friends, our co-workers, and that they've got to be treated like every other American. And I think that principle will win out."

*

"We didn't become the most prosperous country in the world just by rewarding greed and recklessness. We didn't come this far by letting the special interests run wild. We didn't do it just by gambling and chasing paper profits on Wall Street. We built this country by making things, by producing goods we could sell."

*

"There is not a liberal America and a conservative America - there is the United States of America. There is not a black America and a white America and Latino America and Asian America - there's the United States of America."

*

"The Bush Administration's failure to be consistently involved in helping Israel achieve peace with the Palestinians has been both wrong for our friendship with Israel, as well as badly damaging to our standing in the Arab world."

*

"If you were successful, somebody along the line gave you some help... Somebody helped to create this unbelievable American system that we have that allowed you to thrive. Somebody invested in roads and bridges. If you've got a business - you didn't build that. Somebody else made that happen."

*

"We know that the nation that goes all-in on innovation today will own the global economy tomorrow. This is an edge America cannot surrender."

*

"America and Islam are not exclusive and need not be in competition. Instead, they overlap, and share common principles of justice and progress, tolerance and the dignity of all human beings."

"In America, there's a failure to appreciate Europe's leading role in the world."

*

"There are millions of Americans outside Washington who are tired of stale political arguments and are moving this country forward. They believe, and I believe, that here in America, our success should depend not on accident of birth, but the strength of our work ethic and the scope of our dreams."

*

"The United States has been enriched by Muslim Americans. Many other Americans have Muslims in their families or have lived in a Muslim-majority country - I know, because I am one of them."

"We proved that we are still a people capable of doing big things and tackling our biggest challenges."

*

"Tonight, we gather to affirm the greatness of our nation - not because of the height of our skyscrapers, or the power of our military, or the size of our economy. Our pride is based on a very simple premise, summed up in a declaration made over two hundred years ago."

*

"There's something about the American spirit - inherent in the American spirit - we don't hang on to the past. We always move forward... We are going to leave something better for our children - not just here in the

United States, but all around the world."

*

"Today's 24/7 echo-chamber amplifies the most inflammatory soundbites louder and faster than ever before. And it's also, however, given us unprecedented choice. Whereas most Americans used to get their news from the same three networks over dinner, or a few influential papers on Sunday morning, we now have the option to get our information from any number of blogs or websites or cable news shows. And this can have both a good and bad development for democracy. For if we choose only to expose ourselves to opinions and viewpoints that are in line with our own, studies suggest that we become more polarized, more set in our ways. That will only reinforce and even deepen the political divides in this country. But if we choose to actively seek out information that challenges our assumptions and our beliefs, perhaps we can begin to understand where the people who disagree with us are coming from.... The practice of listening to opposing views is essential for effective citizenship. It is essential for our democracy."

*

"We've got some enormous challenges out there.... And I am confident that the American people and America's political leaders can come together in a bipartisan way and solve these problems. We always have. But we're not going to be able to do it if we are distracted. We're not going to be able to do it if we spend time vilifying each other. We're not going to be able to do it if we just make stuff up and pretend that facts are not facts. We're not going to be able to solve our problems if we get distracted by sideshows and carnival barkers."

ABOUT MARRIAGE & FAMILY

"A mother deserves a day off to care for a sick child or sick parent without running into hardship - and you know what, a father does, too. It's time to do away with workplace policies that belong in a 'Mad Men' episode."

*

"I think same sex couples should be able to get married."

*

"I think there are a whole host of things that are civil rights, and then there are other things - such as traditional marriage - that, I think, express a community's concern and regard for a particular institution."

"I think that there's no doubt that as I see friends, families, children of gay couples who are thriving, you know, that has an impact on how I think about these issues."

*

"I opposed the Defense of Marriage Act in 1996. It should be repealed and I will vote for its repeal on the Senate floor. I will also oppose any proposal to amend the U.S. Constitution to ban gays and lesbians from marrying."

*

"I believe marriage is between a man and a woman. I am not in favor of gay marriage. But when you start playing around with constitutions, just to prohibit somebody who cares about another person, it just seems to me that's not what America's about. Usually, our constitutions expand liberties, they don't contract them."

*

"My parents shared not only an improbable love, they shared an abiding faith in the possibilities of this nation. They would give me an African name, Barack, or blessed, believing that in a tolerant America your name is no barrier to success."

*

"I've got two daughters. 9 years old and 6 years old. I am going to teach them first of all about values and morals. But if they make a mistake, I don't want them punished with a baby."

"I don't think marriage is a civil right, but I think that being able to transfer property is a civil right."

*

"With patient and firm determination, I am going to press on for jobs. I'm going to press on for equality. I'm going to press on for the sake of our children. I'm going to press on for the sake of all those families who are struggling right now. I don't have time to feel sorry for myself. I don't have time to complain. I am going to press on."

*

"What I believe is that marriage is between a man and a woman, but what I also believe is that we have an obligation to make sure that gays and lesbians have the rights of citizenship that afford them visitations to hospitals, that allow them to be, to transfer property between partners, to make certain that they're not discriminated on the job."

ABOUT MONEY & TAXES

"In December, I agreed to extend the tax cuts for the wealthiest Americans because it was the only way I could prevent a tax hike on middle-class Americans. But we cannot afford $1 trillion worth of tax cuts for every millionaire and billionaire in our society. We can't afford it. And I refuse to renew them again."

*

"Focusing your life solely on making a buck shows a certain poverty of ambition. It asks too little of yourself. Because it's only when you hitch your wagon to something larger than yourself that you realize your true potential."

*

"This is the moment when we must build on

the wealth that open markets have created, and share its benefits more equitably. Trade has been a cornerstone of our growth and global development. But we will not be able to sustain this growth if it favors the few, and not the many."

*

"I mean, I do think at a certain point you've made enough money."

*

"Now, anybody who thinks that we can move this economy forward with just a few folks at the top doing well, hoping that it's going to trickle down to working people who are running faster and faster just to keep up, you'll never see it."

"The success of our economy has always depended not just on the size of our gross domestic product, but on the reach of our prosperity, on the ability to extend opportunity to every willing heart -- not out of charity, but because it is the surest route to our common good."

*

"If we choose to keep those tax breaks for millionaires and billionaires, if we choose to keep a tax break for corporate jet owners, if we choose to keep tax breaks for oil and gas companies that are making hundreds of billions of dollars, then that means we've got to cut some kids off from getting a college scholarship."

*

"In fact, the best thing we could do on taxes for all Americans is to simplify the individual tax code. This will be a tough job, but members of both parties have expressed an interest in doing this, and I am prepared to join them."

*

"What do you think a stimulus is? It's spending - that's the whole point! Seriously."

*

"We need earmark reform, and when I'm President, I will go line by line to make sure that we are not spending money unwisely."

"We can't get to the $4 trillion in savings that we need by just cutting the 12 percent of the budget that pays for things like medical research and education funding and food inspectors and the weather service. And we can't just do it by making seniors pay more for Medicare."

*

"The fact that we are here today to debate raising America's debt limit is a sign of leadership failure. America has a debt problem and a failure of leadership. Americans deserve better. I, therefore, intend to oppose the effort to increase America's debt."

*

"Now you have a choice: we can give more

tax breaks to corporations that ship jobs overseas, or we can start rewarding companies that open new plants and train new workers and create new jobs here, in the United States of America."

*

"Money is not the only answer, but it makes a difference."

*

"The last thing you want to do is raise taxes in the middle of the recession because that would just suck up and take more demand out of the economy and put businesses in a further hole."

"I want to reform the tax code so that it's simple, fair, and asks the wealthiest households to pay higher taxes on incomes over $250,000 - the same rate we had when Bill Clinton was President; the same rate we had when our economy created nearly 23 million new jobs, the biggest surplus in history, and a lot of millionaires to boot."

*

"I will cut taxes - cut taxes - for 95 percent of all working families, because, in an economy like this, the last thing we should do is raise taxes on the middle class."

*

"Cutting the deficit by gutting our investments in innovation and education is like lightening an overloaded airplane by removing its engine. It may make you feel like you're flying high at first, but it won't take long before you feel the impact."

*

"No party has a monopoly on wisdom. No democracy works without compromise. But when Governor Romney and his allies in Congress tell us we can somehow lower our deficit by spending trillions more on new tax breaks for the wealthy - well, you do the math. I refuse to go along with that. And as long as I'm President, I never will."

*

"But let me perfectly clear, because I know you'll hear the same old claims that rolling back these tax breaks means a massive tax increase on the American people: if your family earns less than $250,000 a year, you will not see your taxes increased a single dime. I repeat: not one single dime."

*

"Unlike my opponent, I will not let oil companies write this country's energy plan, or endanger our coastlines, or collect another $4 billion in corporate welfare from our taxpayers."

*

"We all knew this. We all knew that it would take more time than any of us want to dig ourselves out of this hole created by this economic crisis."

"I can make a firm pledge, under my plan, no family making less than $250,000 a year will see any form of tax increase. Not your income tax, not your payroll tax, not your capital gains taxes, not any of your taxes."

*

"What is a danger is that we stay stuck in a new normal where unemployment rates stay high, people who have jobs see their incomes go up, businesses make big profits. But they've learned to do more with less, and so they don't hire."

*

"I think when you spread the wealth around it's good for everybody."

"When BP was not moving fast enough on claims, we told BP to set aside $20 billion in a fund - managed by an independent third party - to help all those whose lives have been turned upside down by the spill."

*

"The success of our economy has always depended not just on the size of our gross domestic product, but on the reach of our prosperity, on the ability to extend opportunity to every willing heart -- not out of charity, but because it is the surest route to our common good."

*

"When people suggest that, 'What a waste of money to make federal buildings more energy-efficient.' Why would that be a waste of money? We're creating jobs immediately by retrofitting these buildings or weatherizing 2 million Americans' homes, as was called for in the package, so that right there creates economic stimulus. And we are saving taxpayers when it comes to federal buildings potentially $2 billion. In the case of homeowners, they will see more money in their pockets. And we're reducing our dependence on foreign oil in the Middle East. Why wouldn't we want to make that kind of investment?"

*

"When special interests put their thumb on the scale, and distort the free market, the people who compete by the rules come in last."

Dave Farnham

ABOUT WAR & TERRORISM

"I have studied the Constitution as a student; I have taught it as a teacher; I have been bound by it as a lawyer and legislator. I took an oath to preserve, protect and defend the Constitution as Commander-in-Chief, and as a citizen, I know that we must never – ever – turn our back on its enduring principles for expedience sake. I make this claim not simply as a matter of idealism. We uphold our most cherished values not only because doing so is right, but because it strengthens our country and keeps us safe. Time and again, our values have been our best national security asset – in war and peace; in times of ease and in eras of upheaval. Fidelity to our values is the reason why the United States of America grew from a small string of colonies under the writ of an empire to the strongest nation in the world. It is the reason why enemy soldiers have surrendered to us in battle, knowing they'd receive better treatment from America's armed forces than from their own government. It is the reason why America has benefited from strong alliances that amplified our power, and drawn a sharp and moral contrast with our adversaries. It is the reason why we've been able to overpower the iron fist of fascism, outlast the iron curtain of communism, and enlist free nations and free people everywhere in common cause and common effort. From Europe to the Pacific, we have been a nation that has shut down torture chambers and replaced tyranny with the rule of law. That is who we are. And where terrorists offer only the injustice of disorder and destruction, America must demonstrate that our values and institutions are more resilient than a hateful ideology."

*

"I think it is important for Europe to understand that even though I am President and George Bush is not President, Al Qaeda is still a threat."

"With the magnitude of the challenges we face right now, what we need in Washington are not more political tactics - we need more good ideas. We don't need more point-scoring - we need more problem-solving."

*

"We have real enemies in the world. These enemies must be found. They must be pursued and they must be defeated."

*

"In an interconnected world, the defeat of international terrorism – and most importantly, the prevention of these terrorist organizations from obtaining weapons of mass destruction - will require the cooperation of many nations. We must always reserve the right to strike unilaterally at terrorists wherever they may exist. But we should know that our success in doing so is enhanced by engaging our allies so that we receive the crucial diplomatic, military, intelligence, and financial support that can lighten our load and add legitimacy to our actions. This means talking to our friends and, at times, even our enemies."

*

"We've persevered because of a belief we share with the Iraqi people - a belief that out of the ashes of war, a new beginning could be born in this cradle of civilization. Through this remarkable chapter in the history of the United States and Iraq, we have met our responsibility. Now, it's time to turn the page."

*

"Four years ago, I promised to end the war in Iraq. We did. I promised to refocus on the terrorists who actually attacked us on 9/11. We have. We've blunted the Taliban's momentum in Afghanistan, and in 2014, our longest war will be over. A new tower rises above the New York skyline, al Qaeda is on the path to defeat, and Osama bin Laden is dead."

*

"As I've said, there were patriots who supported this war, and patriots who opposed it. And all of us are united in appreciation for our servicemen and women, and our hopes for Iraqis' future."

*

"Of course, violence will not end with our

combat mission. Extremists will continue to set off bombs, attack Iraqi civilians and try to spark sectarian strife. But ultimately, these terrorists will fail to achieve their goals."

*

"For more than four decades, the Libyan people have been ruled by a tyrant - Moammar Gaddafi. He has denied his people freedom, exploited their wealth, murdered opponents at home and abroad, and terrorized innocent people around the world - including Americans who were killed by Libyan agents."

*

"So while I will never minimize the costs involved in military action, I am convinced that a failure to act in Libya would have carried a far greater price for America."

*

"I don't oppose all wars. What I am opposed to is a dumb war. What I am opposed to is a rash war."

*

"I said that America's role would be limited; that we would not put ground troops into Libya; that we would focus our unique capabilities on the front end of the operation, and that we would transfer responsibility to our allies and partners."

*

"We're not going to babysit a civil war."

*

"As a nuclear power - as the only nuclear power to have used a nuclear weapon - the United States has a moral responsibility to act."

*

"For we know that our patchwork heritage is a strength, not a weakness. We are a nation of Christians and Muslims, Jews and Hindus, and non-believers. We are shaped by every language and culture, drawn from every end of this Earth; and because we have tasted the bitter swill of civil war and segregation, and emerged from that dark chapter stronger and more united, we cannot help but believe that the old hatreds shall someday pass; that the lines of tribe shall soon dissolve; that as the world grows smaller, our common humanity shall reveal itself; and that America must play its role in ushering in a new era of peace."

*

"To overcome extremism, we must also be vigilant in upholding the values our troops defend – because there is no force in the world more powerful than the example of America. That is why I have ordered the closing of the detention center at Guantanamo Bay, and will seek swift and certain justice for captured terrorists – because living our values doesn't make us weaker, it makes us safer and it makes us stronger."

*

"The war does not end when you come home. It lives on in memories of your fellow soldiers, sailors, airmen and Marines who gave their lives. It endures in the wound that is slow to heal, the disability that isn't going away, the dream that wakes you at night, or the stiffening in your spine when a car backfires down the street."

*

"All of us have a responsibility to work for the day when the mothers of Israelis and Palestinians can see their children grow up without fear, when the holy land of the three great faiths is the place of peace that God intended it to be, when Jerusalem is a secure and lasting home for Jews and Christians and Muslims and a place for all of the children of Abraham to mingle peacefully together as in the story of Isra, when Moses, Jesus, and Mohammed - peace be upon them - joined in prayer."

"I know that even a successful war against Iraq will require a US occupation of undetermined length, at undetermined cost, with undetermined consequences. I know that an invasion of Iraq without a clear rationale and without strong international support will only fan the flames of the Middle East, and encourage the worst, rather than best, impulses of the Arab world, and strengthen the recruitment arm of al-Qaeda."

*

"We do not have to think that human nature is perfect for us to still believe that the human condition can be perfected. We do not have to live in an idealized world to still reach for those ideals that will make it a better place. The non-violence practiced by men like Gandhi and King may not have been practical or possible in every circumstance, but the love that they preached - their fundamental faith in human progress - that must always be the North Star that guides us on our journey. For if we lose that faith - if we dismiss it as silly or naïve; if we divorce it from the decisions that we make on issues of war and peace - then we lose what's best about humanity. We lose our sense of possibility. We lose our moral compass."

*

"Where the stakes are the highest, in the war on terror, we cannot possibly succeed without extraordinary international cooperation. Effective international police actions require the highest degree of intelligence sharing, planning and collaborative enforcement."

*

"Today we are engaged in a deadly global struggle for those who would intimidate, torture, and murder people for exercising the most basic freedoms. If we are to win this struggle and spread those freedoms, we must keep our own moral compass pointed in a true direction."

*

"It was not a religion that attacked us that September day. It was al-Qaeda. We will not sacrifice the liberties we cherish or hunker down behind walls of suspicion and mistrust."

*

"Al Qaeda is still a threat. We cannot pretend somehow that because Barack Hussein Obama got elected as President, suddenly everything is going to be OK."

*

"We've protected thousands of people in Libya; we have not seen a single U.S. casualty; there's no risks of additional escalation. This operation is limited in time and in scope."

*

"Of course, there is no question that Libya - and the world - will be better off with Gaddafi out of power. I, along with many other world leaders, have embraced that goal, and will actively pursue it through non-military means. But broadening our military mission to include regime change would be a mistake."

ON HEALTHCARE & FREEDOM

"I want to be very clear: I will not sign on to any health plan that adds to our deficits over the next decade."

*

"And that means that no matter how we reform health care, we will keep this promise to the American people: If you like your doctor, you will be able to keep your doctor, period. If you like your health care plan, you'll be able to keep your health care plan, period. No one will take it away, no matter what."

*

"Contrary to the claims of some of my critics and some of the editorial pages, I am an ardent believer in the free market."

"It was the labor movement that helped secure so much of what we take for granted today. The 40-hour work week, the minimum wage, family leave, health insurance, Social Security, Medicare, retirement plans. The cornerstones of the middle-class security all bear the union label."

*

"I know that there are millions of Americans who are content with their health care coverage - they like their plan and, most importantly, they value their relationship with their doctor."

*

"And so our goal on health care is, if we can get, instead of health care costs going up 6 percent a year, it's going up at the level of inflation, maybe just slightly above inflation, we've made huge progress. And by the way, that is the single most important thing we could do in terms of reducing our deficit. That's why we did it."

*

"The fact is, we are closer to achieving [health care]reform than we've ever been. We have the American Nurses Association, we have the American Medical Association on board, because America's doctors and nurses know how badly we need reform.... But look, because we're getting close, the fight is getting fierce. And the history is clear: Every time we're in sight of reform, the special interests start fighting back with everything they've got. They use their influence. They run their ads. And let's face it, they get people scared. And understandably - I understand why people are nervous. Health care is a big deal. In fact, whenever America has set about solving our toughest problems, there have always been those who've sought to preserve the status quo by scaring the American people. That's what happened when FDR tried to pass Social Security - they said that was socialist. They did - verbatim. That's what they said. They said that everybody was going to have to wear dog tags and that this was a plot for the government to keep track of everybody. When JFK and then Lyndon Johnson tried to pass Medicare, they said this was a government takeover of health care; they were going to get between you and your doctor - the same argument that's being made today."

*

"I will never turn Medicare into a voucher. No American should ever have to spend their golden years at the mercy of insurance companies. They should retire with the care and dignity they have earned."

*

"After a century of striving, after a year of debate, after a historic vote, health care reform is no longer an unmet promise. It is the law of the land."

*

"I know my country has not perfected itself. At times, we've struggled to keep the promise of liberty and equality for all of our people. We've made our share of mistakes, and there are times when our actions around the world have not lived up to our best intentions."

"Those who oppose reform will also tell you that under our plan, you won't get to choose your doctor - that some bureaucrat will choose for you. That's also not true."

*

"We will keep the promise of Social Security by taking the responsible steps to strengthen it - not by turning it over to Wall Street."

*

"We have now just enshrined, as soon as I sign this bill, the core principle that everybody should have some basic security when it comes to their healthcare."

"When we think of the major threats to our national security, the first to come to mind are nuclear proliferation, rogue states and global terrorism. But another kind of threat lurks beyond our shores, one from nature, not humans - an avian flu pandemic."

*

"Michelle and I don't want anyone telling us who our family's doctor should be - and no one should decide that for you either. Under our proposals, if you like your doctor, you keep your doctor. If you like your current insurance, you keep that insurance. Period, end of story."

OTHER NOTABLE VIEWS & COMMENTS

"What I worry about would be that you essentially have two chambers, the House and the Senate, but you have simply, majoritarian, absolute power on either side. And that's just not what the founders intended."

*

"We need to steer clear of this poverty of ambition, where people want to drive fancy cars and wear nice clothes and live in nice apartments but don't want to work hard to accomplish these things. Everyone should try to realize their full potential."

*

"The best way not to feel hopeless is to get up and do something. Don't wait for good things to happen to you. If you go out and make some good things happen, you will fill the world with hope, you will fill yourself with hope."

*

"On every front there are clear answers out there that can make this country stronger, but we're going to break through the fear and the frustration people are feeling. Our job is to make sure that even as we make progress, that we are also giving people a sense of hope and vision for the future."

*

"If the people cannot trust their government to do the job for which it exists - to protect them and to promote their common welfare - all else is lost."

"We cannot continue to rely only on our military in order to achieve the national security objectives that we've set. We've got to have a civilian national security force that's just as powerful, just as strong, just as well-funded."

*

"I know that campaigns can seem small, and even silly. Trivial things become big distractions. Serious issues become sound bites. And the truth gets buried under an avalanche of money and advertising. If you're sick of hearing me approve this message, believe me - so am I."

*

"Part of the reason that our politics seems so tough right now and facts and science and argument does not seem to be winning the day all the time is because we're hardwired not to always think clearly when we're scared. And the country's scared."

*

"The Middle East is obviously an issue that has plagued the region for centuries."

*

"If you're walking down the right path and you're willing to keep walking, eventually you'll make progress."

*

"No one is pro-abortion."

*

"We worship an awesome God in the Blue States, and we don't like federal agents poking around our libraries in the Red States. We coach Little League in the Blue States and have gay friends in the Red States."

*

"It's time to fundamentally change the way that we do business in Washington. To help build a new foundation for the 21st century, we need to reform our government so that it is more efficient, more transparent, and more creative. That will demand new thinking and a new sense of responsibility for every dollar that is spent."

"We need to internalize this idea of excellence. Not many folks spend a lot of time trying to be excellent."

*

"We can't have special interests sitting shotgun. We gotta have middle class families up in front. We don't mind the Republicans joining us. They can come for the ride, but they gotta sit in back."

*

"Community colleges play an important role in helping people transition between careers by providing the retooling they need to take on a new career."

"The Internet didn't get invented on its own. Government research created the Internet so that all the companies could make money off the Internet. The point is, is that when we succeed, we succeed because of our individual initiative, but also because we do things together."

*

"In the absence of sound oversight, responsible businesses are forced to compete against unscrupulous and underhanded businesses, who are unencumbered by any restrictions on activities that might harm the environment, or take advantage of middle-class families, or threaten to bring down the entire financial system."

*

"Our combat mission is ending, but our commitment to Iraq's future is not."

*

"After 2014, we will support a unified Afghanistan as it takes responsibility for its own future."

*

"Now we're in the midst of not just advocating for change, not just calling for change - we're doing the grinding, sometimes frustrating work of delivering change - inch by inch, day by day."

*

"It's not enough to train today's workforce. We also have to prepare tomorrow's workforce by guaranteeing every child access to a world-class education."

*

"We want everybody to act like adults, quit playing games, realize that it's not just my way or the highway."

*

"I've said very clearly, including in a State of the Union address, that I'm against 'don't ask, don't tell' and that we're going to end this policy."

*

"It's not surprising, then, they get bitter, they cling to guns or religion or antipathy to people who aren't like them or anti-immigrant sentiment or anti-trade sentiment as a way to explain their frustrations."

*

"We all remember Abraham Lincoln as the leader who saved our Union. Founder of the Republican Party."

*

"We can choose a future where we export more products and outsource fewer jobs. After a decade that was defined by what we bought and borrowed, we're getting back to basics, and doing what America has always done best: We're making things again."

"We have an obligation and a responsibility to be investing in our students and our schools. We must make sure that people who have the grades, the desire and the will, but not the money, can still get the best education possible."

*

"Our friends at the Republican convention were more than happy to talk about everything they think is wrong with America, but they didn't have much to say about how they'd make it right. They want your vote, but they don't want you to know their plan."

*

"With the changing economy, no one has lifetime employment. But community colleges provide lifetime employability."

*

"You can choose a future where more Americans have the chance to gain the skills they need to compete, no matter how old they are or how much money they have. Education was the gateway to opportunity for me. It was the gateway for Michelle. And now more than ever, it is the gateway to a middle-class life."

*

"The thing about hip-hop today is it's smart, it's insightful. The way they can communicate a complex message in a very short space is remarkable."

"So long as I'm Commander-in-Chief, we will sustain the strongest military the world has ever known. When you take off the uniform, we will serve you as well as you've served us - because no one who fights for this country should have to fight for a job, or a roof over their head, or the care that they need when they come home."

*

"Nobody wants to put the creditworthiness of the United States in jeopardy. Nobody wants to see the United States default. So we've got to seize this moment, and we have to seize it soon."

*

"The shift to a cleaner energy economy won't happen overnight, and it will require tough choices along the way. But the debate is settled. Climate change is a fact."

*

"Change will not come if we wait for some other person or some other time. We are the ones we've been waiting for. We are the change that we seek."

*

"We can't drive our SUVs and eat as much as we want and keep our homes on 72 degrees at all times... and then just expect that other countries are going to say OK. That's not leadership. That's not going to happen."

"I don't care whether you're driving a hybrid or an SUV. If you're headed for a cliff, you have to change direction. That's what the American people called for in November, and that's what we intend to deliver."

*

"I'm a warrior for the middle class."

*

"It took a lot of blood, sweat and tears to get to where we are today, but we have just begun. Today we begin in earnest the work of making sure that the world we leave our children is just a little bit better than the one we inhabit today."

"This is the moment when we must come together to save this planet. Let us resolve that we will not leave our children a world where the oceans rise and famine spreads and terrible storms devastate our lands."

*

"People of Berlin - people of the world - this is our moment. This is our time."

*

"A good compromise, a good piece of legislation, is like a good sentence; or a good piece of music. Everybody can recognize it. They say, 'Huh. It works. It makes sense.'"

"In the end, that's what this election is about. Do we participate in a politics of cynicism or a politics of hope?"

*

"Making your mark on the world is hard. If it were easy, everybody would do it. But it's not. It takes patience, it takes commitment, and it comes with plenty of failure along the way. The real test is not whether you avoid this failure, because you won't. It's whether you let it harden or shame you into inaction, or whether you learn from it; whether you choose to persevere."

*

"But the important message I would have for the business community, and this is something that I emphasize every time I have lunch with CEOs, and we have had a lot of them in here, is we have every interest in you succeeding."

*

"I am absolutely certain that generations from now, we will be able to look back and tell our children that this was the moment when we began to provide care for the sick and good jobs to the jobless; this was the moment when the rise of the oceans began to slow and our planet began to heal."

*

"The strongest democracies flourish from frequent and lively debate, but they endure when people of every background and belief find a way to set aside smaller differences in service of a greater purpose."

"All of us share this world for but a brief moment in time. The question is whether we spend that time focused on what pushes us apart or whether we commit ourselves to an effort, a sustained effort to find common ground, to focus on the future we seek for our children and to respect the dignity of all human beings."

*

"You can't let your failures define you - you have to let your failures teach you. You have to let them show you what to do differently the next time."

*

"The best judge of whether or not a country is going to develop is how it treats its women. If it's educating its girls, if women have equal rights, that country is going to move forward. But if women are oppressed and abused and illiterate, then they're going to fall behind."

*

"For all the cruelty and hardship of our world, we are not mere prisoners of fate. Our actions matter, and can bend history in the direction of justice."

*

"No system of government can or should be imposed by one nation by any other. That does not lessen my commitment, however, to governments that reflect the will of the people. Each nation gives life to this principle in its own way, grounded in the traditions of its own people. America does not presume to know what is best for everyone, just as we would not presume to pick the outcome of a peaceful election. But I do have an unyielding belief that all people yearn for certain things: the ability to speak your mind and have a say in how you are governed, confidence in the rule of law and the equal administration of justice, government that is transparent and doesn't steal from the people, the freedom to live as you choose. These are not just American ideas. They are human rights. And that is why we will support them everywhere."

*

"In a global economy where the most valuable skill you can sell is your knowledge, a good education is no longer just a pathway to opportunity – it is a pre-requisite."

"We live in a culture that discourages empathy. A culture that too often tells us our principle goal in life is to be rich, thin, young, famous, safe, and entertained."

*

"Secularists are wrong when they ask believers to leave their religion at the door before entering into the public square. Frederick Douglas, Abraham Lincoln, Williams Jennings Bryant, Dorothy Day, Martin Luther King - indeed, the majority of great reformers in American history - were not only motivated by faith, but repeatedly used religious language to argue for their cause. So to say that men and women should not inject their "personal morality" into public policy debates is a practical absurdity. Our law is by definition a codification of morality, much of it grounded in the Judeo-Christian tradition."

"One of the most durable and destructive legacies of discrimination is the way we've internalized a sense of limitation; how so many in our community have come to expect so little from the world and from themselves."

*

"From the day I took office, I've been told that addressing our larger challenges is too ambitious; such an effort would be too contentious. I've been told that our political system is too gridlocked, and that we should just put things on hold for a while. For those who make these claims, I have one simple question: How long should we wait? How long should America put its future on hold?"